Messianic rabbi, Eric Tokajer has written *Oy! How Did I Get Here?—31 Things I Wish Someone Had Told Me Before Entering The Ministry* as a straightforward tool for the new rabbi, pastor or ministry worker. Don't let the size of this book fool you—it may be short in length, but it is a powerfully practical instrument, like a hammer or screw driver, in the tool belt of anyone who has chosen to obey GOD's call to work in the ministry.

Assembled into 31 easily understood lessons, Tokajer has not only transparently described his own failures, but has given practical steps for the newbie to circumvent the typical areas that can drain a ministry or minister.

I would also venture to say that these life lessons are useful to anyone in a committed relationship with the LORD—whether their work is congregational, para-congregational or in the secular world. More than a worthwhile read, this book will remain a beneficial resource for years to come.

Terri Gillespie Author, *"Making Eye Contact With God"*

"OY! HOW DID I GET HERE?"

Thirty-One Things I Wish Someone Had Told Me Before Entering Ministry

Eric D. Tokajer

MDN
Messianic Daily News
P.O. Box 10943
Pensacola, Florida 32524

"OY! How Did I Get Here"
Thirty-One Things I Wish
Someone Had Told Me Before
Entering Ministry

ISBN 978-0-9894901-6-0

Printed in the United States of America.
The author has made every effort to insure the accuracy of the information presented in this book. However, this information is sold without warranty, either expressed or implied. Neither the author nor the publisher will be liable for any damages caused or alleged to be directly or indirectly, incidentally or consequentially by the use or misuse of any information presented in this book.

All Scripture quoted from the 1917 JPS Bible, Jewish Publication Society, Public Domain

Published by
Messianic Daily News
P.O. Box 10943
Pensacola, Florida, 32524

Front cover design by: Jeremie Webb
Cover Layout: Karen Faire

And combination of great talented friends who put up with me not knowing what I wanted but clearly knowing what I didn't including Robin, Aja, Chase, Karen and Terri.

Dedicated to my wife, Pammy, who managed to stand with me, through all of my failures, while all the time never considering me a failure. Her willingness to allow me to continue to stand back up and start again provided me with the strength I needed.

To my sons, David and Andrew, who somehow survived life in the home of a rabbi while remaining sane and amazingly choose to continue to walk their lives as Jewish believers in Yeshua.

I would also like to thank Robin for her tireless work converting my thoughts on paper into understandable English. It is amazing how much better I sound once her translation work is complete.

CONTENTS

INTRODUCTION

When someone recommended that I write a book, my first thought was who would read it? Why would anyone read a book that I wrote, and what did I really have to share with people that would make a difference? After all, I am truly just an average person.

Then it hit me, there is one thing that I am above average at, "failure." Over the years that I have been in ministry, I have made mistakes, in more ways than I would like to admit. I have learned many lessons from my failures, and maybe it would be good to share some of these lessons learned with others in hopes that they would avoid the mistakes and learn from my failures instead of their own.

Learning from my failures would not only keep readers from going through the pain of learning the hard way. It may also prevent the collateral damage caused during these experiences.

The picture on the front cover demonstrates how I have felt so many times. I cannot count how often I have stopped;

grabbed my head; and screamed, at least inwardly, "Oy! How did I get here?"

Now I know as spiritual leaders we should not think this way, however, we also must be honest and admit that we have.

It seems that just before the "Oy!" moments, everything appears to be going well; life is good, at least in my appraisal of it and suddenly bam!! Almost universal chaos erupts, all around me.

In my ministry experience, I have traveled to many countries. I have helped to lead and/or establish eight congregations, and as I have told many people over the years, I have accomplished making almost every mistake, which can be made. I may not be able to tell you how to do everything; but, I can help you "how not to."

If the only thing that this book accomplishes is a reduction of "Oy!" moments in the lives of those who are trying to shepherd sheep in the Lord's pastures, I will have felt like I have accomplished something amazing and important.

I purposely chose an uneven number for the amount of lessons in this volume because I would never desire for anyone to think this is a complete list of my personal failures. The 31 lessons are just the tip of the iceberg in the lessons I have learned by failure. This volume is only a starting point. However, if each person reading this book manages to avoid one "Oy!" moment, I will feel as if I didn't fail in this effort.

There Is No Power
Without The Power

O ne of the most important tools available to a leader is prayer. However, I have found that many times a leader fails to set aside time to pray and then ends up limited in prayer time by the activities in his life.

Those who need to be praying the most tend to get caught in a trap of praying the least. Our ministry opportunities, which can only be accomplished through prayer, become a catalyst for action. We jump to our feet and head out our door to confront whatever beast is attacking our family, congregants or ministries; and we end up heading out to battle without our weapons and with little or no preparation to fight. It is no wonder we end up defeated, discouraged and disillusioned. Ministry without prayer is very much like a car without gas. It may look great, but there can be no power. It will not go anywhere.

Over the years, I have tried many different methods of praying. As a young believer, I was convinced that the longer I prayed the more effective my prayer life would be. So, I would try to pray extended periods of time each day. These prayer sessions would invariably follow this pattern. First, the excitement of "effective prayer" followed by a short time of prayer, and a longer time trying to think of things to pray about. After I prayed for those things, which were truly on my heart, the rest of the time was consumed with what I can only describe as filler. I wanted to pray for a set time so I did. I found that God answered my prayers because He knew I was sincere, but this didn't mean that I was praying effectively for the whole hour.

I found that most of the time after the pressing issues of the day was prayed; my mind would begin to drift. Even though I was calling out prayers to God, I would catch myself thinking about other things.

After coming to the conclusion that prayer, like most things, is not as much about quantity as it was quality. I changed my method. I began to pray for those things, which were strongest on my heart or in immediate need. I would speak to God as I would speak to someone in authority over me, with simple straightforward words and request. I would pray fervently, but I would not extend prayer for the sake of extending prayer. I found by doing this, I had much more effective prayer time. Moreover, I found that the length of my prayer time grew naturally as I found that there were many pressing things that were important for me to pray about every day. I also found that making time first thing in the morning to pray and get my heart in order allowed me to focus more on the reality of God working things out rather than figuring things out myself.

Once I came to the conclusion that the only way things in the kingdom really get done is by the power of God's Spirit, the more I accepted that my job was to connect with His Spirit, and then let Him minister through me. Without prayer, the best, which we can do, is to try to do what only God can do, then fail over and over.

Prayer needs to be consistent, deliberate and timely.

Consistent: It means you do it regularly. Prayer should become like brushing your teeth. You should always do it before meeting with people.

Deliberate: Because it cannot just be happenstance, prayer needs to be planned and set into motion. In saying this, I know that there are times when a situation arises that time constraints don't allow for preplanned prayer; such as accidents or medical emergencies. These times require immediate prayer. What I am talking about in this chapter is not those emergency prayers. I am talking about our regular daily communication with the Creator of the Universe.

Would you go to the boss's office ill prepared for a meeting? Likewise, we should not come to God that way. Get your prayers organized, at least in your head, and then in a heartfelt deliberate way, share your needs with your Heavenly Father. Remember, He is always waiting to hear from you.

Timely: Because as you learn to have an effective prayer time each day, you will also learn the value of pre-prayer.

Most believers pray after a crisis has arrived on the scene. Once we get in the middle of the crisis event, we then begin emergency prayers to meet the present need. This is like looking for a spare tire after you have a flat. So instead of going from victory to victory, we seem to go from crisis to crisis. However, if you get a spiritual spare time by praying for things before they become problems, life goes along much smoother, and we can live in a victory to victory lifestyle.

For example, you can either pray for a young person not to get involved with drugs before he gets involved or pray for him to be delivered from drugs after he is involved. If we pray first and he remains free from drugs, then we don't have to pray the crisis prayer. The same sentiment applies for all peripheral things people get involved in such as drugs, crime and immoral sex. So you can see that timely prayer is of great value. If we pray before there is a problem, it can keep smaller issues from becoming great emergencies. Effective ministry requires effective prayers. It is not the words, formulas or time involved. It is the consistent, deliberate and timely prayer time that gives us the ability to walk in the realm of world-changing ministry.

You Cannot Remember
What You Have Not Membered

If prayer is the fuel in our spiritual engine, then study is the spark plugs. There is no substitution for opening your Bible and reading it. There is no way you can sustain a successful ministry without daily Bible study. When I talk about Bible study, I mean reading from the Bible. The version of Bible isn't as important as that you open one up, read it, digest it and allow it to become a part of your DNA.

When we study the Bible and allow the Spirit of God to become our personal guide and tutor, we can then share these revelations with others. In other words, you cannot give what you do not have. It is great to read books about the Bible, commentaries and study guides. These are all good tools to make use of as we study and prepare to teach. However, reading books about the Bible is no substitution for truly reading the Bible. It is the difference between personally catching a fish and telling about someone else catching a fish. Telling about someone else catching a fish is a story, but catching a fish is an experience. Our Bible study must be an experience. It should be like exploring an unknown land. Our minds must be sharp and our eyes wide open, knowing that around every bend could be something new and exciting that we have never seen before. Most importantly, we must always follow our guide. No one knows what we might find if we allow God to guide us on our journey through the Bible. After all, He is the author and ultimately He is the only one that really knows what each word, sentence, phrase and story genuinely means.

Like prayers, study must also be consistent, deliberate and timely. Just as we need to eat every day to remain healthy physically, we need to be fed spiritually daily so we can remain spiritually healthy. Just as fast food is generally unhealthy, filling us up for a short time while it does not really provide real strength. We need to avoid fast food Bible study. When possible, dig in for a full sit down dinner and take the time to enjoy it.

Bible study also needs to be deliberate. Setting time aside for study, taking notes and making charts can help to keep thoughts in order. Get a good concordance and dictionary as well as lexicons and varied versions of the text. These resources are easily available for most of us and can really help in our search much like good boots and a walking stick can help on a hike. Another bit of advice is to save your studies; to look back at them later and add to as you get deeper into the Word. You will be amazed how much you will grow in knowledge if you have benchmarks to compare to.

Study should also be timely. When people have questions that you might not have the answer to, you should study right away until you find one. People will not always wait until you find the time to find answers and may go outside of God's Word to look for one. There are also lifecycle and calendar events, which make study and preparation necessary. The amount of time in Bible study is also a quality verses quantity issue. You may spend hours reading verse after verse without veritably studying at all or spend a half hour really digging and mine a real gem. It is not always how long it takes to prepare the meal that make a meal valuable, rather it is the quality of the meal that does.

TO DO MUCH
YOU FIRST HAVE TO LEARN TO DO LITTLE

After reading the last two chapters, this one may seem a little odd to you as I present the case for doing nothing. One of the most important things a leader must do is rest. The ability to stop doing and start resting is difficult to learn especially for those who are in active ministry. We are driven by goals and limited resources. We understand that everything we do is time sensitive. We only have influence on a person's life for a relatively short time. Especially in our rapidly mobile society, so we must press on to fulfill our tasks. We are in a constant state of outreach with building our community, teaching, training and encouraging others. There is always one more opportunity available to us that we just cannot turn down.

If this describes you and your ministry, you need to learn the art of doing nothing, or at the very least nothing involving your job. Ministry is a rare bird. It is the job that has no preset boundaries. Generally, we do not clock in or clock out. No matter where we go or what we are doing, people are watching us. We must always focus on who and what is around. How about at the ball field, the bowling alley? No matter where we are, we may feel we must always be on the job. Well, the truth is living your life that way will eventually allow you to clock out permanently.

Without rest, we will burn out, we will become ill, and we will eventually say or do something detrimental to our families or ministries. Remember always that a wise man said that even God rested on the Sabbath. If we just cannot seem to be able to stop and rest in your town or city, go somewhere else. Take up a hobby, go fishing, play golf, or something fun. Make sure it is something that has nothing to do with working. Stop and smell the roses. Take a vacation. In reality, take more than one. Gather your wife and/or family and go somewhere to just be a family. Have a picnic, go row boating and reconnect with those who love you while they still do!

Do not use excuses like, "I cannot afford it." There are many free or inexpensive things to do with your spouse or family. Pick one and do it. Like the saying goes, "Try it, you'll like it."

YOUR WIFE IS YOUR WIFE

You are on the way into the front door of the bank where you were just hired as the branch manager. The process that led to this day has been long. You went through several interviews; background checks of various types; and finally, you have been hired. You are reporting to work for your first day. As you enter the bank and walk to your new office, you are greeted by a bank board member who asks you, "Where is your wife?" This question seems a little weird, and you reply that she is at home. Somewhat shocked, the board member asks why she did not report to work with you. After all, they thought she would be serving as a receptionist, teller and maybe even an assistant manager.

This scenario seems somewhat far-fetched in the corporate world. It is however a regular event in ministry. It would never be expected that a manager in a corporate position would enlist his spouse to fill all empty positions with the corporation. Yet, it is very dangerous expectation within ministry.

One of the greatest mistakes made by a leader is to ask his

wife to work in a position that she is not gifted or called. I have seen many ministries and marriages fail due to this horrible mistake. A leader's spouse has one primary calling and that is to be a spouse. This is first and foremost her calling. This does not in any way limit her additional callings and gifting. God can and does gift women to work in ministry in many different roles. This does not mean all leaders' spouses have the same gifts.

Unfortunately, many spouses are forced into roles such as administrator, Shabbat schoolteacher, worship leader or any number of different jobs around the congregation. It is true that each of these jobs need to be done. It is not true that the leader's spouse needs to do them. It is just as dangerous to ask someone to do something that they are not gifted in as it is to not allow them to walk in their calling. If your spouse is a gifted administrator, support her. If she is not, fight against any pressure to have her do something that will make her miserable and by extension make you and the rest of the congregation miserable.

Remember, she is your wife and will be looking for you to protect her from this kind of pressure and misery. Pray with her and allow her to be all she is capable of being by the anointing and blessing of God's Spirit. When a husband and wife work together as a team by following God's design, then God is able to bless you in full.

Your Children Are Not In Ministry

I will never forget the first time I asked my oldest son to do something for the congregation, and he told me he didn't want to. The shock I felt bordered on betrayal. How could my son not want to do something for "our ministry?" After coming to myself, I realized that my mistake was thinking that my ministry was "our ministry."

This revelation came to me while I was praying for my son who obviously had in some way walked away from God. What other explanation could there be in his direct and total rebellion against his role as my son? After this truth was revealed to me, my relationship with my children changed. Instead of expecting them to do things, I started to ask if they felt called to do things. This released them to be able to say "no," but it also released them to say "yes" and enter into doing something not because I did expect it, rather because they were chosen by God to walk in their callings. As of today, my oldest son is serving as a rabbi, and my youngest son is active member at the Synagogue that I lead. Each serving not out of my expectations or even the expectations of the congregations they are part of, but because they learned to listen to God and to walk in His callings.

Children are a gift from God. They are family; they are treasures. What they are not is "part of your job." Ministry is a job as well as a calling. Ministry poisons too many children of clergy, because their parents do not separate them from their job. If you were a bank manager, you would not expect your children to spend their free time counting money at a teller window. If you were a pilot, you would not expect your children to work on the ground crew. If you were a surgeon, you would not expect your children to assist you in the operating room. Why do we think that when we enter the ministry our children will assist us at work?

It is shameful that we assume we can enlist our children to do all jobs that come up at our congregations from cleaning and yard work to any administration job that seems to require an extra hand. There is absolutely nothing wrong with allowing our children to volunteer to serve and help in any way they would like to. There is a real problem when we force our children to do something they have no desire to do, just because they are our children.

Our children are an extension of our families; they are not an extension of our job. Why is it that everyone else in our congregation or ministry is a volunteer, but our children are drafted into "service?" The easiest way to harden your child's heart to possible ministry calling is to force them to serve against their heart and desire. Give them the same choice as everyone else you ask to serve. If they choose not to, you can be just as disappointed with their choice as you would anyone else you might have asked. You should not be more disappointed.

Contrary to traditional wisdom, guilt is not the best method to get our children to help. Allowing them to be led to ministry by God instead of pushed to ministry by their parents will result in a personal commitment to serve that will last long after the parent is out of view, and the level of ministry is always higher when performed with a willing heart and real desire.

Don't Save The World And
Lose Your Family

Everyone understands that a call to ministry is a consuming passion. It is not just a job; it is much more than that. As such, we in the clergy can be called out at any hour. Our job is not nine to five. It is twenty-four hours a day, seven days a week. The hope of a standard forty-hour workweek is a dream given up shortly after entering ministry. There is no sense trying to convince anyone that ministry for them will be any different.

With this understanding clear in your mind, always remember that there will always be one more need. There will always be one more person who needs prayer; one more class to teach; and one more lost soul in need of redemption. No matter what your schedule says when you leave for work in the morning, we all know that by the time we get to our first item on the agenda, the schedule is probably no longer valid, and many times the schedule has been reworked a few times. People get sick, accidents happen, and hearts change. All of this is beyond questioning. However, in the midst of all this, the needs outside the home and family are always going to be real needs just as important and just as urgent in your family. Too many times we, as leaders spend so much time outside our homes that we allow our own families to be shredded right under our noses.

I remember a time at a congregation where a ministry was started to work with young men who had gotten in trouble with the law. They were all staying in a youth detention facility. The congregation welcomed these young men into their lives and homes and within a short time; God had really affected these young men. The change in their lives was dramatic and due to the overwhelming transformation they went through, they were given a huge amount of attention. This was noticed by many of the children of the congregation who had been living for God their whole lives, and they soon felt as if the best way to get the attention of their parents and congregation was to be like the young men and have a testimony of deliverance from drugs, alcohol and immoral activities. So, they began to fall away from their dedication to God. The people got so involved with those who were in trouble, that they completely stopped ministering to those who had the wonderful testimony of God's power to keep them from harm. It was only after their eyes were opened due to their children getting hooked on drugs and their young women becoming pregnant that they realized the huge error they had made. It took a long time to repair the breach in their lives. Don't get so busy outside your family that you fail to be the priest of your home.

BODILY EXERCISE PROFITS

I am a well-rounded individual. I have used this and many other "one-liners" to deflect the truth that I was just too lazy to do what I knew to do. I would tell people that they could tell I was on the level because my bubble was in the middle. I would even say because God's Spirit filled believers, being larger meant I had more room for the Spirit. There were even times when I would tell people that the reason I was so large was because people had prayed the prayer of Jabez and my borders had expanded.

The Scriptures tell us that bodily exercise profits a little, but spiritual exercise profits greatly. Unfortunately, many in ministry look at this verse as an excuse to not exercise at all. I can tell you from experience that there are no good reasons not to exercise and take care of our bodies. After the laughter stopped, the truth remained; I was not taking care of the Temple of God. The jokes faded away, but the lack of self-control remained. As people in ministry, we tend to overextend ourselves and not leave time for exercise. The truth is, if we exercise we will be stronger, more fit and able to accomplish more in less time.

Starting the day with regular exercise helps our mind to be sharp, and our awareness becomes greater. If you cannot fit in a time for exercise each day, look for opportunities to exercise during the day. Take the stairs instead of the elevator, park in the farthest parking place and walk into the store, hospital or even to your office. The clergy parking should be the farthest not the closest. Sometimes it is the only exercise we get.

Every day there are many opportunities for exercise if we look for them. Even if all we do is stand up and turn the TV on and off instead of using the remote, it is a start toward a healthier life. Remember we really are to be examples for our flock. Being lazy and without self-control is not a good example of someone submitted to the Spirit of God.

You Are What You Eat, Kind Of

As clergy we should use eating for something other than a good excuse to pray about something. Being in ministry we usually do not have trouble finding opportunities to eat. We tend to eat whenever we meet; we even have special eating meetings after services. We also tend to eat too much fast food, fattening foods and just plain junk food. On top of eating the wrong foods, we also tend to eat too much and at the wrong time of day.

Everywhere we are invited, we are offered food. I don't know how many times I have told people I had to eat a little of everything at a potluck dinner because I didn't want to hurt anyone's feelings. I knew that if I were to honestly tell people that I was trying to eat healthy; they would not have been offended; but, my statement worked as an excuse to eat more than I needed. This led to my becoming what physicians would call morbidly obese rising to a top weight of over 280 pounds. It was only when I couldn't walk up the stairs to my office without becoming out of breath that I woke up to the fact that I was killing myself with food. I also realized that it was hypocritical of me to preach self-control and submission to God while I couldn't bring myself to push away from the table.

Eating healthy does not mean you have to eat cardboard. There are many delicious, healthy foods to eat. I have also found that if while you are praying for God to bless the food you are eating and asking Him to nourish your body; it is also a good time to ask him to help you stop eating when you have eaten enough. In America, we tend to eat super-sized meals and become super-sized people. Eating small amounts of food more often is a good way to keep your body running at peak efficiency. Striving to not eat too late in the evening is also another key to eating healthy. If you eat and then go to sleep, you not only will not digest the food in the best way to process it; you will also tend to have less restful nights.

SAVING NOT BORROWING IS THE KEY

Many years ago when I first entered the ministry I was already married and had one child on the way. I worked a simple, but honest job and made a modest salary. This amount of money was enough to keep our personal bills paid each week with a little left over for extras. If I had saved that money instead of spending it on extras, I believe I would be at least ten years ahead of where I am today financially. In my desire to provide for my wife and children with things today, I didn't really consider the need to provide for them in the future. This doesn't mean that I spent on things that were wrong to buy or that I lived above my means and went deeply into debt. It just meant that I could have saved money early and had things easier now.

Saving early would have provided the ability to buy a house sooner and drive better vehicles over the years. I sat down with my children when they were old enough and I told them. I have made sure you each have a car valued at around $1,500.00. If you are smart, you will drive the car you now have and put the money you would spend on a car payment in the bank. Let's say

$300.00 a month. In a year, you will have saved $3,600.00. Now if you take that $3,600.00 plus your car and trade it on a newer car, you will step up to a little nicer car. Now with that, continue to bank the $300.00 a month for the next year and you will again have $3,600.00 in the bank plus your great car. If you choose to trade again, you now have a car worth around $4,000.00 plus the $3,600.00 so you can see how you can step up each time. If you follow this process for five years you can buy a new car every year if you choose to and never pay interest on a car your whole life.

This idea of delayed gratification is one I wish someone had taught me when I was eighteen. The same idea can be applied to homes and other items. Think of all the money we each would save in interest payments alone if we chose to save now and pay later instead of buy now and pay later.

Another way of saving money that is easy to do and very effective: use coupons. Our synagogue has a coupon swap every other week and people save hundreds of dollars a month by using them. Also, don't be too proud to shop at thrift stores, or online discount retailers. Every dollar you save using wisdom is a dollar you can use for your family.

Two People In Trouble
Is Not Better Than One

S ome years ago I took a course to become an EMT (Emergency Medical Technician). One of the highlights of the class is what they called "practical scenarios." These scenarios were used to see how we would handle different events. The teacher would let us know what we did right and help us to correct our mistakes; it was a very effective hands-on teaching method.

One of the first of these practice scenarios was an automobile accident. We "arrived" on the scene and saw a three car collision with victims in all three vehicles. The first response from those on our unit was to rush to the site of the accident and triage the scene. We ran from car to car checking the people and following all the instructions we had been given in class. We finished our job and stood proudly to the side. It was only then that our instructor informed us that we had all died shortly after leaving our ambulance. The one thing we didn't do was access the scene of the accident to make sure it was safe for us to enter.

This particular scenario had one of the cars crashing into a power pole. The result of the car hitting the pole was a hot power line had been broken free and was on the ground electrifying the car, which we had quickly touched while trying to rescue the passengers. In our desire to rescue someone who was in trouble, we would have ended up dead ourselves.

I tell this story because I cannot count the times in ministry where I acted to assist someone only to place myself in a position where I then needed help. Many times people asked for financial assistance, to which my response was to reach into my wallet and give them some money. The amount of money I gave would usually only cover part of the need they had, but it was all I could do at the time. Later that day, I would go home to find that a bill I had was due or that my family needed groceries. Having given away the money, I depleted the available cash for my bills. The conclusion was that not only did the person who came with the need not leave with enough money to meet their need, but now I also didn't have enough money to take care of my need. By reacting to the situation, I didn't check if the scene was clear, and in the end, we had two people in trouble instead of one.

This isn't to say we shouldn't try to help those in need. Ambulance crews arrive on the scene to help; they just won't put themselves in danger to provide it. If the paramedic gets hurt while trying to provide care, who is there to help the paramedic? If the paramedic is hurt, there is no one to help the original injured person.

The same thing happens in spiritual situations also. If you are not prepared by praying, fasting and studying, the scene is not safe for you to provide care. I have caused more congregational problems by jumping into a situation and reacting instead of prayerfully responding to them. It is also important to remember that it takes a long time for both the person in need and the "rescuer" to recover from bad care.

TEACH WITHIN YOUR ABILITY

When I was a cub scout, I was so excited to be going on my first ever camping trip. Having arrived at our camping location deep into the woods, we started to set up camp. Our troop was as busy as an ant colony working feverishly clearing the area; setting up tents; and preparing locations for the all-important campfire. As I began to set up my area, I pulled out my never before used tent and all the other brand new camping supplies my mother had bought and started to set everything up. Having never camped before, this process was already difficult. Adding to this level of difficulty, due to my already full-grown male ego, I would not ask anyone for help.

Trying to appear that I was an experience camper, I worked until my tent was up, and my gear was loaded into the tent. I am not sure even today how the tent remained standing throughout the weekend. It was at this moment that my fellow scouts decided to take advantage of my swelled ego, and after looking at my area showed me how I had failed to take into account the direction of the wind flowing across the fire. I was going to either have to rework my entire tent or find a "smoke shifter."

They then kindly suggested who I might ask to borrow a smoke shifter, so that I would not have to take down and reset up my already sad looking tent. I spent the rest of the afternoon chasing a very illusive "smoke shifter" from area to area.

Now most of you reading this today know there is no such thing as a "smoke shifter." Had I been willing to simply admit that I didn't know what one was and ask someone to help me find it, I would have found out the truth early on. This lesson stayed with me all of my life. That is not to say that I never allowed my ego to overwhelm my intelligence and cause me to find myself in an embarrassing situation again.

In ministry, we often find ourselves being asked questions about the Holy Scriptures that we may not have either any understanding or a complete understanding about. These opportunities will either make or break your standing with those who are in your sphere of influence. At the moment when you realize that you don't have a good answer to a question, stop immediately and let the person know that you don't know the answer. Let them know that you would be more than happy to look into the question and find an answer. Don't act ashamed of your lack of knowledge in an area; only one Man had every answer for every question in the Bible and that was only because He wrote it. Once you have committed to find an answer for someone, follow up and give them the answer. Ask friends, study, read commentaries, whatever you have to do, and then let them know you did what you said you would do.

Another thing to realize is that the time and effort of studying, you still may not have a definitive answer to a question; believe it or not that is okay also. Just make sure that when you share what you have searched out, you let the person who asked know the results of your research, but that even after all that, you are still not sure about the answer you have come up with and that you will continue to search and get back to them.

IF IT IS TRUTH PREACH IT

One of the joys that I have had over the years is to be invited to speak in many different congregations both Jewish and non-Jewish. As I shared with these diverse groups of people, I usually allow a time for a question and answer period. These forum sessions can be the most powerful part of an outreach presentation.

When I first began to have the meetings, I would begin with prayer. As I prayed aloud for the meeting, in my mind I would ask God to speak to the hearts of the people and not let them ask any questions which would be too controversial or cause me to hurt the feelings of those in attendance. Almost without fail, one of the first questions would be about a topic that was a hot button issue. At first, I would use a very political approach to answer the question. By circling the questions with a combination of Biblical quotes and amusing answers, I would avoid the complex issue that might bring offense.

After doing this for some time, I began to feel guilty about it. If what I believed was truth and someone asked me about my beliefs, why should I not openly and honestly answer their questions? Now this does not mean that I do everything I can to be abrupt and offensive with my answers; it does mean that I use grace to share truth openly.

Truth is truth. We don't need to defend it. We need to present it to all of those who will listen. When given the opportunity to share in different places, respond in love and grace but be honest in doing so. Remembering that the most hateful thing we can do is to withhold the truths of God's Word from anyone.

When a child wants to play on the highway, we do not allow him/her to do so because we don't want to see them get hurt. We do everything within our power to explain the dangers of playing on the road, and then if that does not work, we will even place ourselves in danger to attempt to pull them off of the roadway. There is no difference when it comes to false teachings and doctrines. The conclusion of a false foundation is the destruction of the house.

We should never hold back the truth in any forum or meeting no matter what we think the cost to us might be. Remember true love causes us to lay down our lives for others.

CHECKS AND BALANCES

There is more teaching about finances in the Scriptures than almost any other single topic. More leaders get into trouble due to financial issues than almost any other problem. It is vital to your ministry that you insulate yourself from this type of problem. Remember, even the appearance of mismanagement can destroy a ministry. I know it is difficult, especially at the start of a ministry, to not be involved with handling money for your ministry. However, at the first possible moment remove yourself from the sole role in record keeping and banking. Soon assign someone else to either write checks or use a double signature program.

At our congregation, this is how we have things set up: when we receive money, a group of three people count the money and record it in two separate formats, one hard copy in a record book and one on a computer program. The money is then sealed in an envelope and the three people sign across the seal. Then another three people get together early in the week usually on Monday and verify the signature on the seal; open the envelope; and recount and verify the totals. They then enter the total into the bookkeeping program that our congregation uses making sure the totals all match. Photocopies of all checks are made, and the deposit is recorded. A copy of the deposit slip, the photocopies of checks received, and the original envelopes as well as any envelopes that were filled out with cash donations are stapled together with the bookkeeping record sheet. Once the deposit is made, the deposit receipt is then stapled to the packet already assembled. This process implements a "check and balance" system throughout our record keeping. From the first time the money is counted until it is in the bank, we have no less than six people with three different written records to check and balance against each other.

Another aspect of this process is that I, as the leader, am not involved in the counting and record keeping of the donations. This allows me several freedoms. First, nobody can claim I took any money that I should not have. I don't touch the money; so I cannot be accused of mismanagement or misdirecting funds. Second, and just as important as not handling the offerings, I am insulated from knowing the amounts given by members of our congregation so when teaching or preaching I am not swayed by the fear of losing a "Big Giver" by what I am saying. I don't know who gives what amount so all people are on a level playing field in my mind. This also helps when dealing with inter-congregant issues. I cannot be accused of or tempted to take someone's side because of the amount of money they give.

Additionally, I am not a signer on the general fund checking account of the congregation. A member of the finance committee signs all checks. Again, this allows me great liberty from accusation, if I can't spend the money I cannot be accused of misspending it.

With all of this being said I do know the financial standing of the congregation and require accurate reports of accounts receivables and payables. I also receive reports of members who stop giving regularly. Not the amount given but the constancy of giving. This is a one good barometer of the spiritual health of a member of the congregation. It also helps us to interact early if a problem arises. When a regular giver stops, there is a problem. It could be they are upset with the leadership. If they are, this gives an opportunity to confront the situation and seek restoration quickly. They could be having financial problems, and this also allows for the congregation to become active in assisting them through the situation. Again, this is not information about the amounts of giving but a change in consistent giving.

The leader is and should be accountable for the financial health of the congregation, but they should also do everything within their power to protect the congregation from attacks due to the involvement of the leader with the congregation's money.

TRUST THOSE GOD SENDS TO HELP

Most ministry leaders have a real parent-child relationship with their congregation or ministry. As with any parental relationship, it is difficult to leave your child in the care of another person for the first time. It is even more difficult to allow someone to care for your child for a long time.

I remember after the birth of our oldest son, my wife and I were encouraged for our sanity to find a babysitter and go out for an evening by us. Being wise enough to know good advice when we heard it, we contacted a trusted friend and set them up to watch our little boy while we went out for dinner. I watched my wife as she spent the entire time while we were at dinner looking feverishly at her watch every few seconds. This went on for less than half an hour before she could not take the separation and worry any longer. I finished what food I could as she got ready and off we went to check on the baby. Of course upon our arrival at home, the baby was perfectly fine sleeping soundly and didn't seem to have missed us in the least.

In ministry, we tend to have the same attachments to our flock that we, as parents have toward our children. This tendency can be as dangerous to our ministry as it can be to our family. Our ministry will only grow as large as the foundation is allowed to grow in supporting it. If we want to control and look after every part of our ministry, we can expect to have only a micro ministry. If we allow those who are brought to our ministry to walk fully in their gifts and talents, our ministries will grow in effectiveness. This is not to say that we leave our baby with anyone that comes along. It does mean that those who clearly have a calling to work with us should be allowed freedom to walk out their calling. It is hard to learn to let go and allow people to grow in their ministry roles. By definition, it means we need to acknowledge that those helping will not be perfect and will many times make mistakes large and small. This is how we learn, and this is how they will learn.

If we believe that our ministries will belong to God, then we have to believe that we are really not a parent who needs to be worried about our baby. Instead we are the babysitter watching over His baby. Once we understand this truth, we can more easily make the jump to understanding that just as God trusts us to walk in our calling; we must trust those who God brings into our lives that they too will mature into their calling.

Raise-Up People Slowly

As a leader, we are required to raise-up and train other leaders. You don't let a teenager drive a car without some training. Likewise, we don't allow someone to step up to a leadership position without some training and much prayer. I once heard a man I respect greatly share a message entitled "It is easier to appoint than to disappoint." Another way to say this is that once you have placed someone in a position of leadership; they become a part of the foundation stones of your ministry. Once they are in place, it can be difficult, but not impossible, to remove those stones without causing some destruction to everything standing upon them. It is for this reason we are warned against raising novices up to positions of authority too quickly (I Timothy 3:6). Now, I understand that in context this verse is directly relating to bishops. However, I believe that by extension it can be faithfully applied to all leadership offices.

People can have great energy, enthusiasm and have a wonderful desire to be active and involved with everything. Sometimes we as leaders can mistake their excitement for calling. Too many times, we are so busy trying to do everything, to reach our communities that we use anyone that is willing to step into a position.

I like to play golf. It is one of those things in life I find both challenging and relaxing at the same time. In addition, it is one of the rare times when my cell phone is turned off. If you could see me drive up to the first tee, you would see someone that looks like a golfer. I have an excellent set of clubs, a golf shirt, golf hat, golf glove and golf shoes that are all professional looking. I even use good golf balls. However, no matter how much I look like a golfer, am excited to play, and know the terminology, the truth is I am a novice golfer. If you really wanted to win a tournament you would not want me to be on your team. Even though I have all the looks and enthusiasm to play, and might even hit a great shot on the first tee, underneath the trappings of a professional golfer, I am still a novice.

This is exactly the same with people in ministry. Many times a new person will come to our congregation. They will be totally sincere about their beliefs, and God will have totally transformed their lives. In other words, they are not faking their experience at all. They are excited about serving God and have zeal to work in His kingdom. They will volunteer to do anything. To any leader this is a wonderful thing because in the average congregation ten percent of the members do ninety percent of the work. Anytime someone will step up, we want to use them. With this said, the Scripture clearly warns us not to appoint leadership positions to those who do not have practical life experience to balance their zeal. Otherwise, just as my golf ball spends more time in the weeds than in the fairway, your ministry will also spend much more time in the weeds than on the greens. We cannot confuse "availability" for "ability."

Remember, it is easier to appoint than to disappoint. Allowing someone that may truly have a calling to serve too soon can lead to a premature "burn out" due to jumping into ministry too early. This will not help you, them or your congregation in the long run. The Scriptures tells us to watch and pray. This should be used when appointing leaders. First, watch them for a while. While praying for them, mentor them and let their gifts make room for themselves.

SOMETIMES IT IS BETTER
NOT TO HAVE SOMETHING

This was one of the hardest lessons for me to learn in ministry. When I looked at the successful ministries around me, I would see all the activities they had going on, and I equated their success with their programs. So I started to encourage programs. We started a youth program, a married program, an outreach program, a prison ministry, a hospital ministry with many other programs in between. We rushed into doing all of these things. Because after all, time is short, and we do not know how much time we have left, either in this life or before the world to come.

What we quickly found out is that having really bad programs rushed together with little training and even less gifting, does not equal success. We ended up with a group of ministries trying to work with very little budget and work force. Many of the same people were involved with more than one ministry; this brought up divided loyalties and divided time. Because we didn't really have the finances to support all the growth in programs, everything was done on the cheap, which caused very little positive results both in outreach and in the growth of the people who were involved in the ministries. Instead of each ministry feeling as if they were important, each one ended up feeling like a redheaded stepchild, all fighting for their piece of the chicken.

This is not to say that to be successful you have to always spend extensive amounts of money. What I am saying is that we should do everything as unto God, and this alone should cause us to reevaluate the programs we have. Anything worth doing is worth doing right. Not, anything worth doing is worth doing any way you can.

LET PEOPLE DO THEIR JOB

One of the best ways to make people not want to do anything in your congregation is to micromanage everything you give them to do. If we really believe that a person is called to do a job, then it is up to us as leaders to let them do it.

One of the best examples of micromanaging a job is the example of King Saul and the young man who would become King David. A large, big-mouthed and arrogant Philistine was causing Israel problems. There was a need, and King Saul asked for volunteers to meet the need. After a while, David arrives to apply for the job. Saul checks his credentials. David has, by this time, killed both bears and lions while protecting his father's flock. So, King Saul appointed David to slay Goliath.

Now remember, King Saul was not planning on doing this job himself. He had the opportunity to do so and chose not to. The next thing we read is that King Saul does want David to kill Goliath; however, he wants him to do it his way. King Saul gets his armor, his helmet, and his weapons and puts them on David.

After looking himself over, David realizes what a mistake it would be for him to try to fight using King Saul's armor, especially since he had never fought that way before.

In a commendable way David lets the King know that if he wants him to do the job; he needs to let him do it his way. Remember, David is not asking to do something other than what King Saul had asked him to do. He is not asking to do something that would be wrong to do; he is not asking to go over budget in performing the job. What he is asking is that King Saul would allow him to do what he asked him to do without managing every aspect of the battle.

We all know that King Saul listened, and as a result, David defeated Goliath and delivered the Israelites from the enemy. Once you have appointed someone to serve in a position, and have given the limits of the job, then back away and let them do the job they were chosen to do. This will allow a twofold positive conclusion. First, it will allow them to grow in faith and confidence in their calling. Second, it will allow you the freedom to work in your calling.

THINK TWICE ACT ONCE

For several years, I worked in a plant which built prefabricated framing for roof truss systems. My first day on the job I learned two very important lessons. First, there is no such thing as a camber reverse rod, even though I spent the better part of the day walking around the plant from section to section chasing one while people continued to direct me to the person that had just left their area with it.

For those who don't know, Camber is the natural bend in a board. Every board has a natural camber even if it looks straight to the eyes there is a slight bend in every board. The second great lesson I learned that day was to measure twice and cut once. After cutting a large group of two by fours the wrong length because I had misread the measurement, I was strongly encouraged to not let it happen again by a very large and very loud supervisor. I learned this important lesson the hard way.

This lesson does ultimately cross over to ministry. Before you do anything, think it through; pray about it; discuss it with others that you respect; and if possible, seek counsel from others who have experience in the area of ministry. Only after spending time in preparation and planning and then re-going over everything, embark on your project. This will not guarantee success in your project, but it will guarantee your project will be a success.

You can plan for a fishing trip and bring everything required for a good trip, and still not catch any fish. Failure to plan and to make sure you have brought everything needed, will guarantee failure.

CHOOSE YOUR BATTLES

When I first started in pastoral ministry, I was very motivated in my zeal to make sure that I was seen as in charge and having authority. I was not long into my new role that I realized that I was spending a great deal of time fighting battles to prove my position of authority. After expending more effort proving I was in charge instead of just being in charge, I realized that there were two kinds of battles. Ones that you have to fight to win and ones that you can win by not fighting them.

I know this might seem like a weird thing to say. After all, how do we win a battle by not fighting? The answer is simple. Let me try to explain with two examples.

Example one: we had a man in our congregation who was in a leadership position and had suggestions concerning our service. I could have debated all the ins and outs of why I would like the service to follow a different format. However, this was not an issue where I had strong feelings or felt as if something he was suggesting was out of order spiritually. So we made changes according to his suggestions.

I have seen leaders choose to use times like this to impose their authority as the leader and make changes just to show who is boss. Instead of fighting a battle with this man and taking the risk of making an enemy, I chose to not fight this battle and save using my authority for a time when it would be needed more.

These decisions should be based upon a set of standards that will answer these questions. First, "Will fighting the battle make any difference in the long run?" Second, "Is this issue significantly spiritual, for the health of our congregation?"

Example two: as we grew as a congregation, we decided to allow those with different talents the opportunity to serve the congregation. One of the ways we chose to do this was to ask some members of the congregation to open our service by greeting the people, saying a short prayer and making a few announcements. We initially had asked three people to serve in this capacity. Two were men and one was a woman. The three of them rotated in this job, and all three did an excellent job.

Shortly after instituting this new program of ministry, I had a man and his wife, come up to me and tell me that they didn't like the idea of a woman being on the platform. I explained to them what the roles of these people were and that there was nowhere in the Scriptures that prohibits women from serving in this way. They replied that it made them feel uncomfortable, to which I replied that in this case once every three weeks, they would be uncomfortable.

I know this may seem harsh to you, but this was an issue that could have turned into a cancer. It would cause division and could even destroy our congregation. I had to choose to fight this battle, and I had to stand in authority. The difference between these two possible battles is that the first example would not change anything one way or the other, and the second battle could have destroyed a whole congregation. By the way, that family continued to attend our congregation for years and still visits when they are in town.

NIP IT IN THE BUD

Many years ago I watched one of the most insightful TV programs I have ever seen. If you have had more than thirty birthdays, I am sure you have at least seen glimpses of the Andy Griffith show. One of the characters in the program was Barney Fife, the faithful sidekick of the wise and knowing Sheriff Taylor. Barney's weekly antics and wild ideas require Sheriff Taylor to bail him out of trouble. Throughout each episode, Barney, while causing chaos, is always sharing wisdom with all those around him. Even when everything is falling apart around him, Barney would share homespun wisdom with those constantly watching him miss the mark. Just because Barney was not able to follow his own wise advice, doesn't mean we should not work on following his advice ourselves.

One of Barney's tried-and-true expressions was that problems needed to be "nipped in the bud." In other words, when a situation first becomes apparent, just as when a plant first buds, if it doesn't look fruitful, we need to nip it. Cut it away from the plant.

The more we work with people, the more opportunities there will be to follow Barney's advice. Too many times for one reason or another, we see a "bad bud" begin to grow in our congregations; and we do not handle them quickly and decisively. It may be that it is an influential congregant involved, such as your wife or husband. I assure you once a bud is formed; the longer it is growing, the more damage will be done to the plant. The proper response to a "bad bud" is not to ignore it and hope it goes away. The only proper response is "Bud Nipping."

SAY YOU'RE SORRY AND MEAN IT

We live in a world that has all; but has left the idea of personal responsibility behind them. Everything we read in the newspaper; watch in theaters or see on TV teaches us that nothing is ever our fault. Our problems all arise from other people's actions, and if we just had better homes, more money, more education, etc., our problems would be solved. You can look far and wide before you will find someone that will admit they made a mistake.

If we are going to be good leaders, we are going to have to learn that we have to admit that we make mistakes, many mistakes. The sooner we learn this fact and own up to it, the better we will get at fixing the mistakes we make.

One of the things I have learned over the years is that if you fess up, most people will accept your apology with a handshake or a hug, and relationships will be stronger because of it.

The key to a real apology is not just to say you are sorry but to genuinely be sorry. When you are truly sorry about something, you will do everything possible to change what was done. Don't try to joke it away, don't try to split the blame, and don't try to make an excuse. Just take responsibility for the problem, error, mistake or purposeful choice; admit it; and change it. My sons would say it is time to put on your big boy pants and be an adult. People will not learn to repent if we don't show it in our lives in front of them.

A few years ago, I was very excited when three different friends asked me to participate in special events in their lives. Two of the events were weddings, and the third was a speaking opportunity at a special once a year event. Each event was important, and each person was special to my family and me. There are few greater joys as a leader than being chosen to be involved in these kinds of events. The only problem was that I gladly accepted each invitation without consulting my calendar. You guessed it; these three events were at the same time. To make matters even more difficult, all three events were in different states.

When I found out what happened, I was very overwhelmed. I didn't know what to do. Those that know me know that this was not the first time I double-booked my schedule. For several years, almost every gift I received was a day planner, phone message pad, calendar and even a Palm Pilot. This was, however, the first time with three unique events in three different states, scheduled for the same time. After I prayed a bunch, I called each one of them letting them know that I had made a huge mistake and asked them to forgive me. As it turned out, two of the events ended up changing times, and I was able to go to all three events. This was only one of the many errors which I have made over the years. This was not by any means the worst mistake I have made.

Engage Your Brain
Before Your Tongue

For seven years, I worked in construction. I owned a company that installed doors and windows. Most often, we installed in new homes, but we also did installations for people remodeling their homes. In construction work, there are some rules that help you get the job done and make money while doing it.

I don't know how many times I heard a supervisor or superintendent tell a new worker to make sure they measure twice and cut once. I also cannot tell you how many times I heard someone shout out on the job "I have cut this board four times and it's still too short."

My experience with building materials helps me to understand that words can cut more dramatically than a saw can. As a leader, thinking before speaking is not just suggested practice; it is required practice. As a congregational leader, we must always consider the situation before saying something. We also need to consider how we are going to say what needs to be said. My first thought before speaking to anyone is not, "What should I say?" it is, "Should I say anything?" Only after deciding if saying something is needed comes the question of what to say.

My father helped me in many ways to think before speaking. One of the lessons my father taught me had to do with my oldest brother. Let me start by saying I was the youngest boy in a blended family of eight children. One of my older brothers had a temper, and because he was older and stronger, he would tend to bully the younger children to get his way. I had hoped that as he got older this downward flow would stop. However, it wasn't until one year when my father allowed my brother to buy a motorcycle things changed.

Now, in our home, every privilege was two sided. I was very young when I realized that it seemed we were only given privileges so that our parents had something to take away from us as a punishment. In the case of my brother's motorcycle, with the privilege of owning a motorcycle came the new understanding that any imposing of will by bullying would result in immediate prohibition of motorcycle privileges. My father instructed my brother that if he needed to he should count to ten before saying or doing anything. I noticed that the word motorcycle had exactly ten letters. Whenever my brother would begin to say or do anything that would violate the "no bullying" rule, I would tell him to count to ten, m-o-t-o-r-c-y-c-l-e.

This lesson has stuck with me throughout my life. Before I speak, I stop and count. I then think, "Does it have to be said?" If the answer is no, then I don't say anything. If it is yes, then I stop again and think about how I would want to be told whatever it was I am about to say. Then, and only then, do I say something. I can tell you the damage done by not engaging your brain before your tongue is often more problematic than trying to stretch the board to the right measurement after cutting it to the wrong length.

PASTORAL PRIVILEGE
IS A SHIELD NOT A SWORD

A very important idea in pastoral work is the idea of pastoral privilege. For those unfamiliar with this term, it is a legal privilege that allows for private communications between clergy and congregant to remain confidential. This allows for clergy to be able to freely communicate with their congregants and counsel them, in order to help them to overcome weaknesses or issues in their life.

Pastoral privilege is a shield to protect the congregant from open ridicule that might result from personal failures or problems in their life. Unfortunately, some leaders have chosen to use private information communicated in confidence as a sword instead of a shield of protection. I have known of leaders who would use this kind of information to manipulate and control their congregants. The evil done to people in this way is horrific because not only are they hurt by the breach of trust, but they also may lose confidence in all spiritual leaders and never trust a leader to help them again. Everything told in confidence should remain in confidence. I know many leaders who share things like this with their wives and do so with permission of those they counsel. We should never take advantage of the confidence and trust of those who come to us for help to control or manipulate people to do what we want or take our side in situations.

Leadership by definition requires followers. People choose to follow a leader simply because they are leading. There is no surer sign that you are not a leader than the fact that you have to push people to follow you. By the way if you are pushing, you are not leading.

Don't Expect People
To Really Hear What You Say

For some reason, we feel that people should give us their undivided attention all the time, but understand that we don't always listen to them as they speak. I say this with all honesty; I have a very difficult time paying attention to people when they speak to me. If they don't get to the meat of the matter in a hurry, I am no longer in the room with them. They may be leading up to a very important topic that is vital to them and their lives. If I don't know what it is in a hurry, I am gone. I may be there in the physical, but I am thinking about the study I am giving the next day or a Bible passage that had me puzzled. I may be thinking about a couple that I have been counseling and the crisis they are going through, or it may be my grandchildren and what we are going to do together the next time we see them. I may even think of something super spiritual, for example what I plan to eat for lunch when our meeting is over.

I am sure that I am not the only person whose mind wanders and takes trips while people are speaking to me. The thing to remember is that while all of this is happening, and while I am traveling to the distant planets of my world, the people that are speaking to me are directly in front of me, and looking directly into my eyes as they speak.

Now imagine the other side of the coin; people whom we are speaking to have the same issues we do. They are listening to us with about the same level of attention as we offer them. Add to this equation that many times what we say is something difficult to hear personally and emotionally, or difficult to understand theologically. Then add to that, those we are speaking to are listening through a filter of their understanding, their personal history, their personal experience and boom! No wonder we say something, and they hear something entirely different! Communication is much more about making sure people hear what we say, and then it is about how well we say what we say.

Too many leaders share important information with the unrealistic expectation that the receivers heard and understood what they said. I know this is a difficult thought for us to hear, especially since much of what we do is accomplished by talking to others, either individually or in groups. This is why it is so important that we present information in ways that keep people present. They not only have to be with us, they have to be "with us."

We need to prioritize what we have to say and prepare to say it in a way that people will receive it. This is easier to do when speaking to individuals, because you can tailor your words to a particular person's interests and education. This can be more challenging when speaking to a group. It can be challenging, but not impossible. The key is to first provide a central interest point to the people and then focus on it, through your time talking.

People do not have to come to hear you; they are already interested in what you have to say. It is not only possible; it is necessary for us to provide something to interest them. It is up to us to keep them interested enough in it to hear what we have to say.

IF THE BOAT IS SINKING

Almost everyone has seen what happens to a boat once holes are punched in it. We grew up watching cartoons of a row boat in the middle of the water. The adversarial character sneaks up with a drill and quietly drills holes in the bottom of the boat. When this happens, we see the water sprinkling up in the air like little lovely fountains, and the hero of the cartoon starts to try to plug the holes. You know a finger here, another finger there; a toe over here, etc. It is interesting that I have never seen a cartoon character more interested in finding out who drilled the holes.

In ministry, we will find ourselves in a constant setting of being in a boat while an adversary sneaks up to drill holes in it. It will be our natural leadership nature to try to find the cause of the holes; who is to blame; and how can we stop them from ever drilling holes in our boat again. We drop to the ground, in panther stalk mode and begin our search for the villain. We grab our pipe and magnifying glass and start following footprints tailing the scoundrel, leaving no leaf unturned in our efforts to find and blame the perpetrator. All the while, our boat is sinking fast and all of those aboard it, including ourselves, are speedily descending into the murky depths.

How many people have we allowed to drown simply because we were busy looking for who put the holes in the boat, instead of clogging up the holes? In reality, it doesn't matter what caused the holes until they are fixed. Once the passengers are safe, then it is time to search for the cause of the holes.

I have watched over the years as leaders tried to get to the bottom of a problem. They allowed finger pointing and accusations, "He said; she said" to go on. While watching the boat sink, they did nothing to patch the holes. With each moment, the water gets deeper, and the pressure causes the hole to get larger. With each minute, the damage gets more pronounced, and the hurt becomes harder to repair.

When I was young, I played little league baseball. As with most teams of young boys when our team was winning, we tended to all love, honor and respect one another. However, as with all groups of young boys when our team wasn't winning, we would start to argue, complain and in many cases, fight with each other. The coach's first action was not to ask who started it; whose fault it was; or even to become the judge of the situation. His first response was to have the boys shake hands. Why? If they were shaking hands, the fight was over. The hole was plugged. Then, the coach would pull both boys aside and find out what caused the hole. You see he understood that if he immediately tried to find the cause it would only allow for continued fighting or even more holes to be drilled. I didn't realize what a wise man he was until I had to start dealing with fights myself.

THERE CAN BE ONLY ONE

When I was a young person, I watched a movie that although I don't recommend watching it now, has been a very important precept in my life, both in secular management and in ministry. The movie's plot is about beings that are immortal except if they were beheaded. They could only be killed in battle by losing their heads. When one was beheaded, the other immortal gained the power and strength of those that they killed. The conclusion of the movie is after all other immortals were beheaded, there would only be one immortal left alive. The tag line repeated throughout the movie after each immortal was killed by another immortal, "There can be only one."

In my job whether ministry or secular work, there can only be one leader. The leader can have assistants and helpers, but ultimately there has to be one leader who directs the path of the organization and implements the vision. Too many leaders try to govern by poll, or worse, allow those serving with them to undermine their authority and usurp their role and function. The end of this type of management is the same as in the movie;

eventually someone's head has to roll. It will either be the leader or the person who has challenged the leader, but at some point, there will be only one clear leader.

If you are going to be an effective leader the first thing you must do is to decide you are going to be the leader. Not *"a leader,"* but *"the leader."* This should be established at the beginning. If it is, life will be easier for you. This does not mean that everyone will accept your leadership, but it does mean that if they don't accept they are choosing not to be a part of completing the vision with you. If you are already in a position where you have not established your leading role, make it a point to do so. Not as tyrant, but instructionally, be clear, be firm and be honest. It may take an apology for not being the leader you should have been, and a statement that from now on that you will be. It is a wise saying that "anything with two heads is a monster, there can be only one!"

KNOW THE DIFFERENCE BETWEEN "THERE" AND "THEIR"

One of the most common problems in writing is the misuse of the words "there" and "their." One of the most common problems in ministry is also related to those two words. The word "there" has to do with location; the word "their" has to do with relationship.

One of my favorite Biblical verses that demonstrates this difference is Exodus 24:12,

> *"And the Lord said to Moses, 'Come up to Me into the mount and be there; and I will give you tablets of stone, and the Torah and commandments, which I have written, that you may teach them.'"*[1]

You notice here that the Lord tells Moses where to be "into the mount" that is the "there" and then the Lord tells Moses to "be there" and that is the "their." I know in my years of ministry, I have spoken to people and not really been there. I have been at events and not really been there. We all have done

---

[1] 1917 JPS Bible

this. Our bodies were present, but our hearts and minds were elsewhere. We all have heard someone say, "The lights were on, but nobody was home." This is what I mean by the difference between "there" and "their." If we are truly going to be able to influence people's lives, we need to start acting relationally instead of locational. It is not enough just to be present; we must really be intent on being connected personally.

It is one of the hardest things to accomplish. Just think about it this way. Moses was about to visit with the Lord, the Creator of Universe, and he even had to be reminded to "be there." We visit people at their homes, in hospitals and other places. While we are with them, it is easy to drift into thoughts about what else is on our schedule; a crisis either taking place or about to happen; or even what our spouse or children will be doing that day that we are missing because we are where we are. However, no matter how tempting it is to let our minds and hearts travel, we cannot be successful in ministry unless we are not only "there but also 'their.'" Remember Moses was about to receive the tablets from the Lord, so he could share them with the Children of Israel, and in His invitation to Moses, He reminded Moses he had to "be there."

DO YOU HAVE AS MANY POMEGRANATES AS BELLS?

Around the bottom hem of the High Priest's outer garment was a row of alternating bells and pomegranates as an adornment. As most readers know pomegranate is a tasty type of fruit sometimes called "the fruit of Kings." The seeds of the fruit are the part consumed and enjoyed.

Almost everyone has enjoyed the sound of bells at some point in their lives. Bells can get our attention, as a dinner bell does. They can also be used for warning signals. Many naval vessels, throughout history, have used bells. However, bells when sounded too often or continually can become extremely annoying and painful to the ear.

When I first started serving as a congregational leader, I noticed how often my messages each week seemed to speak of the prophetic warnings of Daniel, Isaiah, Ezekiel and Revelation. Often I felt like Jonah preaching about devastation coming upon all those who fail to repent and turn to the ways of the Lord.

One day a revelation about sermons came to me, almost in a quiet voice in my mind. I realized one of the reasons I focused on judgment messages was because I didn't have enough fruit to preach about. I had many bells but few pomegranates. Once I changed my focus of ministry to have a balance of showing fruit and sounding bells; I saw an increase in attendance and excitement for what we were doing as a congregational community. It is only by having equality between bells and pomegranates that we can have pure religion.

Those of us who serve in ministry leadership roles have the obligation to let the bells sound. We need to share the message provided to us in the Holy Scriptures with all those who will listen. We need to sound the alarm, and we need to get people's attention. Unfortunately, too many leaders have demonstrated the bells without demonstrating the fruit. It is vital that we remember the pattern of alternating bells and fruit.

Leaders must demonstrate the fruit of relationship with the Lord as much as the warnings of the Lord. We all know those who shout from the rooftops that destruction and judgment is coming. It is important to note that this is true according to the Bible. This message of judgment must be balanced with the message of love and forgiveness, hope and redemption. While bells by their very nature make noise that is heard by those all around, those who crack into them and see the seeds within only enjoy pomegranates. The point I am trying to make is that while we are preaching righteousness like Noah, we need to be equally transparent in sharing the fruit that the Lord has brought forth in our lives. Bells are used to alert people to needs, but it is the fruit that provides for those needs. For those who would like to see your congregations grow, remember that growth comes from planting seeds, and bells don't have seeds.

HONESTY IS NOT THE BEST POLICY

One of the most painful lessons in my ministry had to do with honesty. It was through that experience that I learned that honesty is not a policy. It is a commandment. You may ask what the difference is. Well, this is simple. If it is only a policy, then policies can be changed as time goes on. Every circumstance and situation can bring adjustments to the policy. With policies, we have options. With commandments, there are no options. We do not have the choice of situational observance. When honesty becomes a commandment to us and not policy, we learn humility, patience, long suffering and more than all of that, we learn to think about the impact of what we are going to say before we speak.

Many years ago, I lost a great friend, because I said something that was untrue. To my knowledge, they have still not fully forgiven my actions and choice. The impact of what happened affected hundreds of lives and relationships. The short story was my family had a need; I sought out help for the need; and a dear friend provided the help. When I asked for the help, I was very honest and open about the need, and my ability to restore the person that blessed me, and my family by helping. Over the time in which I had committed to make good on my obligation, unforeseen events changed my circumstances. With those changes, I continued to be honest about what had happened. However, at some point, for reasons I cannot explain even today, I twisted the truth in my responses to my friend, and the twisted truth eventually became a lie. This lie in hindsight was never necessary as the truth, though uncomfortable, might have strained our friendship but not ended it.

This lie deeply hurt my reputation. The result of this policy of honesty was a division of friends as some chose to stand by me and some chose to stand by the person who had so kindly blessed me with help and whom I had hurt profoundly.

Most people are not dishonest because they are trying to hurt people. They start out with the truth and as time and events change, they fall into the trap of justifying their untruthfulness with the hope that what they said would become true before a crisis erupts.

In my case, my words were an attempt to delay until the provision I was expecting arrived, and I could keep my word by restoring what was given to me. I had talked myself into believing that things would be better if I could just appease my friends' growing impatience until I could fix everything. In truth, an honest answer would have appeased my friend. Looking back I see how much they loved me and my family to help as they did. From their displayed actions, the truth would have clearly been better although still uncomfortable for all of us.

Please don't fall into the trap of progressive deceptions. Don't believe the lie, that a little lie won't hurt anyone, or that you are protecting someone by lying to them. Every lie diminishes your credibility and your reputation. It will destroy not only your relationship with people, but also your relationship with the Lord. Honesty is not a policy. It is a commandment.

AVERAGE IS EXCELLENT

As a young leader, I spent much time watching other people who were leading ministries to see what they were doing and how they were doing them. This process can be very healthy as it allows for establishing and setting goals. Observing others who are doing similar ministry to what you envision will allow you to see what works and doesn't work and can assist you in allocating resources especially your valuable time.

A pit that we can fall into while doing this observation is to start comparing success and failures. Simple comparisons are not the danger I am warning about. Once we begin to establish in our mind what we believe successes and failures are, we begin to live our lives and our ministries jumping from mountaintop victories to valley failures. While all of this jumping tends to make our lives exciting, it also causes leaders to miss out on many triumphs that we fail to perceive, because our lens are focused wrong.

Let me give you some examples that may help to make my point clearer. When we started our congregation at our first service, we were so thrilled to see almost forty people in attendance. It was beyond our expectation, and we really were happy to have such a response. The second service was not quite as well attended as we dropped down to around twenty attendees. Our initial limits were established "forty = victory" and "twenty = failure." As time went on, we continued to grow, and our average attendances continued to grow along with the years. Today, if we only had forty people show up for service, we would consider it a distinct failure. As we grew, our expectations of what success was grew also, and our perception of failure also changed. This is a very natural way of thinking, and every leader I know does this type of comparison.

However, the problem with this type of rating system is that we constantly are looking at opposing ends of a spectrum for what success or excellence is. While doing this, we usually forget to live where we are. We fail to notice that our average today is usually higher than our goal of yesterday. We are so busy chasing the next mountain that we miss out on the beauty of the mountain we are standing upon. You see, when attendance is forty, sixty is a great goal. When we reach sixty, one hundred is within view, etc. As leaders, we do too little to recognize the accomplishments that lead to our current average. In doing so, we fail to remember that today's average was yesterday's excellent. This trap not only affects the leader who is constantly chasing something just ahead and out of reach, it also affects those who are making the journey with us, because they do not receive the accolades for their efforts to reach excellence. Always remember, "Today's average is yesterday's excellent."

Don't Do The Right Thing

I cannot tell you how many times someone asked me why I was going to do something which I clearly didn't want to do. My answer was, "It is the right thing to do."

As leaders, we need to be very careful about our motivation, for doing the things that we do. What we do is not about just doing the right things; it is more about doing them for the right reason. Too often, we can become almost robots serving our congregations with the same effort, thought and motivation that we put on our shoes. The "service" becomes a response instead of a purpose.

We counsel and advise; we visit people in jails and hospitals; and we teach classes and preach messages. I have at one time or another done each of these tasks and many others, because I was able to do them and not because I desired to do them. When I speak of desire, I am not speaking of ambition or a mere impulse to do an assignment; I am talking about a spiritual calling and direction from above. We as spiritual leaders have the one vocation available, in which doing the right thing, just because it is the right thing to do, is not enough. Too many leaders burn out and give up on their calling, because they become disconnected from their calling.

Those who you are serving are not looking to your leadership, because they want someone to do something for them. They are looking to you as a leader. Leaders do not just do things; they connect people to a greater vision and plan. Every event, every message, every lesson and every instruction must be leading the sheep you are shepherding to the next pasture. It is not enough to just feed them where they are, they are looking to you to bring them to tomorrow and the next day. If you do not continue to be connected to your vision or your spiritual compass "GPS," your ministry will cease, and a job will begin. Bitterness, envy and jealousy will result. Not envy of other people, but envy of what you once dreamed you would accomplish. So don't just do the right thing, do the right thing for the right reason.

85683125R00070

Made in the USA
Lexington, KY
03 April 2018